Rehoboth

Abel Andarge

authorHOUSE®

AuthorHouse™ UK Ltd.
500 Avebury Boulevard
Central Milton Keynes, MK9 2BE
www.authorhouse.co.uk
Phone: 08001974150

First published by AuthorHouse   12/9/2011

ISBN: 978-1-4670-1322-2 (sc)
ISBN: 978-1-4670-1323-9 (e)

CONTENTS

PREFACE

What motivated me to prepare this specific document, are the turbulent situations of the world.

Nowadays, the chaotic situation of our world is the source of great concern. In addition to various natural disasters, there are also several tribulations caused by human beings. Some of these natural and artificial problems of the world are air pollution, deforestation, draught, starvation, malnutrition, diseases, lack of medication and health care, human right abuse, oppression, conflict, war, terrorism, crime, and so many other physiological, psychological, social, political and economic problems.

Even though it is impossible to hundred percent eradicate these problems, it is indeed possible to challenge them in a better condition.

In order to save our world from the above problems, and the like, the unity of its peoples is decisive.

We, the human race, have the ability to think and measure things unlike other animals and creatures. Hence, the responsibility of evolving our world in to a better place to live in rests with us. We would be able to discharge our responsibility provided that we tolerate and respect one another.

If wars were the solution to our problems, the wars fought in the world so far would have brought changes in our favor. We have learnt from our history so far that measures of force and war would bring about more disastrous situations rather than solutions. If we are wise, we can observe and obtain a lot of lessons from the situations of the world in the same manner as we would be in schools. We can judge by considering our current situation, by considering our surroundings and reading and listening about the past history of the world.

The management system of our world requires reorganization. This reorganization is to come about through peaceful means instead of through clashes. There is no problem that cannot be solved by dialogues.

We human beings require dialogues based on mutual understanding, respect for one another and love for one another.

In order to solve the problems of the world, we need to start with the endeavors of solving the problems of our own respective countries. The endeavors should begin in countries and then should evolve into continents and eventually the world.

Even though endeavors are to begin in our respective countries, our vision should mainly be extended to the world. It is rather foolishness to love one's own country and have hatred towards the continent in which the country is found.

Doing ill to other countries for the good of one's own country would culminate in doing ill to one's own country. When the world is damaged in one way or another, not only the human race but also other living creatures would be damaged. This is rather futile and even more futile than following the wind.

What meaning would it give for a person to destroy the base and to decorate the wall? Would this action make the person rational or a meek or a foolish?

If we wish to unite the world, we need to work a lot in the sector of Social Science. The world is registering a lot in terms of technological advancements. There are astonishing inventions and developments in building construction technology, transportation technology, medical science, electronics engineering, computer technology and space science etc.

However, we have not been able to register as much solutions as we need for Social and political issues of our world. Considering the fact that politics has been entitled as Part of Social science, those concerned should find solutions in the same manner as formulas of scientific findings for the world's problems.

Not only politicians but also teachers and students of all social studies should work day and night to suggest solution for the complicated political problems of the world.

I am a Social Science student and I believe I should actively participate in the endeavors geared towards the reformation of the world. In this respect, I always think of solutions that would solve the problems of my nation, the continent of Africa and that of the world. The main purpose of this document is to give responses to the question which developmental path would bring about change of better developments to the Ethiopia and similar developing countries without any conflict and commotion as well as War. And to suggest that the unification of the world should be implemented as soon as possible.

Ones upon a time, my respected instructor Dr. Ermias Abebe gave me an assignment. The assignment was to recommend a developmental stratagem Ethiopia should adopt for the realization of development. The title of the assignment was "Peaceful Developmental Revolution for Ethiopia" and its main purpose was to give responses to the question which developmental path would bring about change of better developments in the under developed countries without any conflict and commotion as well as War.

This assignment proved to be one of the most favorite assignments given to me so far. The reason is because I had the opportunity to express my imaginative proposal. I would like to express my gratitude to Dr. Ermias for this opportunity.

Consequent to my belief that fast development can be achieved in Ethiopia bringing about radical change entirely free of any conflict whatsoever, I have submitted this peaceful developmental proposal.

This paper contains spring board proposals for international unity peace and security. Let us embark on the main topic. I wish you a pleasant reading.

CHAPTER ONE
DEVELOPMENT FOR ALL COUNTRIES

Development of a country is the same to development of a state. It means the assurance of better administration systems and existence of better ways of living for the people in the state. When we say better administration, we mean that for every human being, in an individual level, the accessibility of every essential obsession for life and basic needs setup to provide him/her with all human rights for which he/she is entitled, such as pure air, pure water, sufficient food, clothing, shelter (housing), health care, education, job, sufficient rest, security, justice, peace, freedom, amusement physical exercise (sport), moral and ethics, social interaction, possibility of reproduction (access to establish family), and so forth.

Beyond these conditions, a human being deserves to live in a clean and beautiful environment with as fewer plights as possible; and everyone ought to be able to get benefit from the discoveries of modern technology in a manner which harmonizes with nature. Technology should not contradict against nature rather; human being is supposed to synchronize technology with nature so that all discoveries of technological inventions can benefit not only the human race, but also other animals and creatures that are at least non-harmful for humans, as well as the earth with its helpful constituents in general.

If a state is able to provide with the aforementioned conditions suitably to all the individuals within the state or at least to the greatest number of the people, it means that the state is developed; but if the state is unable to provide with those things and conditions appropriately, it means that the state is not developed.

As development is relative, there can be neither a perfectly developed state nor absolutely undeveloped state. Rather, it is common to find a certain extent of development within an undeveloped state and it is also usual to get some aspects of underdevelopment in a developed state. Nothing is absolute in this world. Relatively, a state which provides the above mentioned elements in a higher amount, compared to a state which provides with them in a lesser amount, can be considered as the <u>more developed</u> state; whereas, a state which provides them in a lesser amount, compared to a state which provides with them in a higher amount, can be considered as the <u>less developed</u> state.

For the state development two essential things are required:
1. Availability of natural resources
2. Proper management

The first one, availability of natural resources means useful things provided to mankind naturally or artificially such as land, favorable weather condition, water, biodiversity, livestock, farm products, minerals, and so on.

The second, proper management means good administration of man power and resources.

It accounts for the existence of an administration system capable to provide the available resources and services fairly to all of the state members (individuals) and to assign all the skilled people on the right job as per their ability.

Knowledge, wisdom, information, skill, fairness, justice, peace, good governance and so many other things related to humanity and aptitude of human being are included in the issue of proper management of man power and resources.

Although there are various types of political ideologies in the existing states of the world and every ideology is prepared to maintain the above mentioned things, the ways and strategies of maintaining that of development differ one from another.

When we consider the state development, we are referring to the institutional state. A State is an institution; however, even if the state is considered as an institution (organization), it can't exist separated from other similar organizations (states). In our world the existing states must work together for the growth of the world in solidarity cooperation and unity.

Our planet Earth is the collective home of mankind; therefore it is our main organization. We ought to achieve its security and progress. State development cannot be considered separately from world development. Any care and caution exerted to preserve the states must be related to universal benefit.

DEVELOPMENT FOR ALL CONTINENTS

Our earth is divided in 7 continents and except for the Antarctic, in the rest 6 continents people are living. These continents are the sub organizations of the earth. Therefore, it's possible to assume that we have 6 big organizations. All populations must work for the growth of their continents. The Asians must develop their continent without adverse effect to others, the Africans must develop their continent without adverse effect to others; the Europeans must develop their continent without adverse effect to others; People living in Australia North and South America must enrich their continents without harming the others as well. Let all peoples of all countries adopt the vision of a better and developed world.

The 6 continents are divided by political boarders due to mankind. These divisions would be tolerable if they could provide a better administration. But if they result in conflict, segregation and boarder turmoil degenerating in full scale war entailing hate and racism, the prejudice is higher. These artificial boarders are being more and more numerous from time to time. That is how today in our world there are about 196 independent countries. There are even 54 countries in our continent Africa only.

DEVELOPMENT FOR AFRICA

Currently in Africa, the issue of unity is a major discussion topic. Leaders of African countries meet periodically to discuss the ways and means to reinforce their unity.

As division, conflict, war and similar problems have injured the continent of Africa for centuries, unity is the most profitable solution in order to overcome such troubles and to maintain development in a continent level. Any African should think about the development of the continent of Africa. The African peoples and governments should develop their continent in a manner which is not prejudicial to others. Let us join together to insure peace, security and growth for our continent.

The African growth cannot be considered separately from the one of the World. Africa is part of the world and it is needed not only for Africans but also for non Africans. To solve the problems of Africa, the primarily responsibility lies on Africans and secondly on non African peoples.

So as to solve the problems of the continent, Africans must start to operate from their own countries. Every African must first develop his/her own country. While mainly focusing on African growth, any step to enrich our own country ought to be encouraged. Each action taken to develop ones country in Africa must be related to the interest of the continent and to the interest of the world ultimately.

All 54 African countries, peoples and governments must relate any activity aimed at developing their own counties, to the continental development and ultimately to the world at large.

CHAPTER TWO
2.1 The Flawed Developmental Scheme

Since some governments are striving to develop their own countries, being devoted to the advantage of their country, they commit aggression against other nations and states. Everywhere boarder conflicts, wars and invasions are breaking out. For this reason, even if the mightier government seems to have the upper hand for a certain period of time, finally it is injurious to the continent and ultimately the world.

As it disrupts world peace in the long run, it is not beneficial to any one and because it is destructive to mankind, it cannot be considered as a success history.

The practice of building nations and states while demolishing the continents, or building the continents while demolishing the world is useless for anyone but it is distractive for humankind. That is flawed developmental scheme.

Governments and peoples striving to develop their own countries without harming other countries should be appreciated as their activity is constructive for the world. And that is admirable activity.

Therefore all countries, governments and peoples must work for a better world instead of attacking and killing each other. When peoples and governments are committed to the developmental issues of their countries, they should be more committed to the development of their continent; in that manner, they ought to be more and more committed to universal progress.

2.2 DEVELOPMENT OF A COUNTRY
TO ENRICH THE WORLD

Although the practices for development of a country are the liability of each citizen, governments are more accountable for this duty. All peoples and governments must rise to develop their countries and eventually to generate a better World.

In order to build a better world, countries must operate in reciprocal respect and understanding. Hence, to make the world a better place to live in, the crucial mission of countries must be reciprocal respect and understanding.

Down with exploitation, oppression, violation, conflict, terrorism, and war.

2.3 OPTION BUT NOT OBJECTION

The effort that the Ethiopian government is currently making to develop the country is encouraging. As far as my views are concerned, it is the responsibility of every citizen to develop the country not only by reflecting ones interest of support but by collaborating practically with the government as well.

Each Ethiopian citizen has to stand alongside the government for one objective. And this objective is to bring Ethiopia out of its current backward situation and to take it to a better stage of development.

I do support the development activities the Ethiopian government is carrying out both by theory and by practice.

Why I am writing this totally different proposal is not to oppose the development programs being undertaken by the Ethiopian government, but to present an alternative idea that will make our country superpower in a fast moving development which will not take long time (not more than one year). This proposal is an alternative idea not an opposition to the Ethiopian government development programs. The initiating of alternative development theories and promoting same is the right of every individual which the Ethiopian constitution approves. Since government is a body which interprets the constitution properly, I hope it will give its optimistic decision by looking into this proposal.

2.4THE NEW POLITICAL THAUGHT

I am about to introduce you to my new vision of development initiated by Ethiopian and American context.

My first objective is to perform a quick development to my country and more over to provide a benefit to Africa and the rest of the World ultimately. I start from Ethiopia to submit discussion proposals to generate a better world and solutions for the existing problems. Therefore, I have a thought to secure the swift development of Ethiopia and to reach a higher stage of growth.

My thought can be considered at two levels. The first one is the Starting Point and the second is the Objective. In this short text, the first section which is the Starting Point is to be presented; that is called "STATE MERGE APPROACH".

2.5 STATE MERGE APPROACH

The objective of this approach is to put the World under the leadership of one state.

By the mergers to be carried out among developed countries with developing countries and by mergers of developed countries among each other. In this approach, the time frame for Ethiopia to become the first developed country of the World is the term required to implement the proposal which is only one year. As a result of implementation of this proposal, Ethiopia is defiantly supposed to be a super power and the first developed country of the world within the period of one year time (within 365 days only).

This approach is not only useful for Ethiopia but also for the United States of America which is today a supper power. Because, it will help the USA go further in terms of political, social and economic power and preserve its unity.

This plan begins with proposing a new grand merger to be carried out between Ethiopia and United States of America and establish a reorganized great state.

So as to realize this approach, the adoption of the theory by the two governments of Ethiopia and USA to implement it must be acquired. The scholars of the USA and Ethiopia are expected to convince governments to practice the proposal.

2.6 HOW FAR IS THE LIMITATION?

Does this approach serve only to the union to be made between Ethiopia and US-America or can it be applied to other countries?

The State Merge Approach is beneficial not only for US-America and Ethiopia. It is an approach that can be applied to countries found in any continent or in any part of the world. This approach encourages the mergers to be carried out by all countries and particularly highly encourages mergers to be carried out among developed with developing countries, secondly it encourages merging to be carried out among developed countries as well.

In this modern era, we are living in the prevalent of modern transportation and communication equipments which are the results of modern science and technology; the distance of place and remoteness will not pose any problem among countries willing to merge.

Therefore, the merger to be made based on political economic and administrative conditions is more successful than the merger to be made on the basis of existing geographic proximity of countries.

When developed and developing countries make a union, the developed countries can become successful as they will get additional land, natural resource, human resource and political success.

And the people found in non-developed countries, as a result of the union, will have the opportunity to get better access for food, shelter, clothing, health care, education, employment, good governance opportunities, and the like, they become successful. Therefore, the main objective of this approach is to enable developed and undeveloped countries to merge and secondly it is to make merger between two developed countries.

When two developed countries merge, since they will form a larger institutional state having a huge political and administration structure, aside from their power being strengthened highly, it will decrease the military power confrontation being currently evidenced among superpowers. And this will have positive contribution for peace of our world.

Therefore, on the basis of this stipulation, scholars and governments of any country studying this approach and synchronizing it with the objective realities of their own countries can put it into practice.

CHAPTER THREE
The Relation Between
Ethiopia And U.S. - America

I found the following article from the internet website in 1, August 2008. I supposed it helps us obtain basic information about the relation between Ethiopia and America and wanted to present it as it is.

Source: - "CELEBRATING OVER ONE HUNDRED YEARS OF ETHIOPIAN-UNITED STATES RELATIONS" ....*http://www.africa-ata.org/ethiopia-usa.htm*

While almost all of Africa remained under colonial rule or was still being explored by Europeans, a formal relationship was established between Ethiopia and the United States on December 27, 1903 by Emperor Menelik of Ethiopia and Commissioner Robert P. Skinner representing President Theodore Roosevelt of the United States. For centuries, Ethiopia remained suspicious of colonial powers that were continuously and actively engaged in the exploitation of Africa's vital resources and people. Ethiopian leaders found the United States to be far removed from all centers of colonial exploits and as far back as 1863, Ethiopian leaders made inquiries about the emerging nation on the western side of the Atlantic Ocean. They were excited and wondered whether they could, one day, align themselves with such a powerful nation in order to restrain European and Middle Eastern intrusion to acquire and bequeath land that rightfully belonged to Ethiopia. Emperor Menelik, the architect of the Ethiopia-United States relationship, saw the United States as a counterbalance to the European powers whose design was to weaken and eventually colonize his country. Thus the initial treaty between the two countries representing a truly historic diplomatic document was signed, known as the "Treaty of Amity and Commerce", which accorded Ethiopia the status of "Most Favored Nation" (MFN) and consequently led to full-fledged diplomatic relations.

In subsequent years and decades, Emperors Menelik and Haile Selassie showed strong interest in the immediate promotion of Ethiopia's unique relationship with the United States. Ethiopia was once a superpower that played a significant political and economic role on the world stage. Its international ties extended to the far corners of the world. Over its long and storied history, Ethiopia prided itself on its great achievements in socio-political organization, arts, literature and science, as well as innovations in agriculture and engineering. Being an ancient civilization, Ethiopia among other things gave coffee and numerous grains and plants to the world. The foundation for this unique relationship was perhaps laid on the eve of 1896, when Ethiopia successfully stopped the European scramble for Africa at the gates of Adwa in northernmost Ethiopia. Indeed, it was this principled opposition to both European colonialism and totalitarianism that made the United States a natural and trusted ally of Ethiopia. Known as a country with a long history of independence, potential for trade, geographical significance and endowed with raw materials, Ethiopia definitely caught the attention of U.S. policy makers. These characteristics provided a stable background for the evolution of what would be a mutually beneficial, strategic convergence of interest between these two countries: Ethiopia, one of a few countries that can claim continued existence and history of over a millennium, and the United States, one of the youngest and most dynamic nations in the world. By and large, successive leaders of both countries have been keeping this important fact at the forefront of their foreign policy making.

It is truly remarkable that the substance of this strategic partnership and shared destiny between the two countries has remained constant over more than a century. For instance, the United States greatly appreciated the support of Emperor Haile Selassie's moderating influence on the formation of the Organization of African Unity (OAU) now known as the African Union (AU). Likewise, Ethiopia stood behind the United States in its effort to strengthen the United Nations as a peace broker. Ethiopia participated in crucial peacekeeping and peace making missions in several hotspots of the then Cold War world. Through time, Ethiopia became a major recipient of U.S. economic, technical and military assistance. The United States helped with the consolidation and strengthening of the air force, navy and army, making the Ethiopian defense forces perhaps the best in sub-

Saharan Africa, able to repulse any foreign-backed domestic insurgencies and external invasions alike. Over the century, there has been a deeper understanding and appreciation of the historical, geopolitical and strategic significance of the bond between the two countries. Moreover, more than one million Ethiopian-Americans are working very hard to revitalize and energize a greater Ethiopian-American friendship by building bridges that connect the two peoples ever closer. The vital interests of both Ethiopia and the United States have been kept alive and forged in times of both peace and adversity, and it is the fervent belief of many Ethiopians and Ethiopian-Americans that the United States, as in times past, will stand by Ethiopia as the two nations continue into the next one hundred years of an enduring partnership.

Source: - "CELEBRATING OVER ONE HUNDRED YEARS OF ETHIOPIAN-UNITED STATES RELATIONS" ....http://www.africa-ata.org/ethiopia-usa.htm

** As we have seen it, Ethiopia and USA have a long standing relation. This good relation should be developed to ultimate unity level for absolute union and that would be advantageous for both countries. When the union is realized, United States of Ethiopia will be established.

According to this new proposal, U S A and Ethiopia will be merged to form one great state and amendment of their denominations will be performed so as to make the name of the state more inclusive. That name will be <u>United States of Ethiopia.</u>

CHAPTER FOUR
4.1.1 United States Of Ethiopia

The United States of Ethiopia accounts for the enlargement of the good relation between USA and Ethiopia towards ultimate unity by which they would build one great state.

This unified state encompasses the two countries; and its governmental system, legislation, regulation, directive and over all political structure must continue on the basis of the current structure of the USA. All of the today's Ethiopian regional states whereas American's local states are to be administered by one central government. The Future supreme state will include the present Nine Ethiopian Regional States with the two City Administrations (Addis Ababa & Dire Dawa) plus the fifty local States of USA.

In the United States of Ethiopia every local state will have its own governor accountable to the central government and president. When this state is established, the central government will give new citizenship to the present American Citizens and the present Ethiopian Citizens. In other terms, the overall American people and Ethiopian people will be citizens of United States of Ethiopia. Any US Ethiopian citizen will have a social security Number and his/her own residence permit ID Card. Any one holding this ID card can travel, live and work freely all over the territory of US. Ethiopia.

4.1.2 NUMBER OF THE LOCAL STATES

At the time of the union, is the current Ethiopia to become one local state and added to the 50 local states of America? Does it mean generally there will be 51 States? Or are the current regional states of Ethiopia to continue as they are now?

At the time of the union, the number of the local states will not be only 51. The current Ethiopia will not change itself into a local state. At that time, the current 9 regional states and the two administrative city councils (Addis Ababa and Dire Dawa) totally the 11 states (Regions) will continue as local states and will become accountable to the central government.

At that time each of the current Ethiopian regional state will be administered by the similar internal structure by which the 50 US-American states are currently administered. And they will become accountable to the current US-American central government which will be then called "The Central government of United States of Ethiopia."

The US-Ethiopia local states number will be 61 incorporating the 50 current local states of US-America and the 11 local states (regions) of the current Ethiopia.

Until such time in the future when US-Ethiopia invites other states to become part of its territory and until other nations and states put requests for similar union, the local states of the United Stated of Ethiopia will be about 61.

The current US-American government will continue its activities by becoming in the future the US-Ethiopia central government.

The capital city of the State and the seat of the President will be determined following diversified studies and discussions to be made in the future. US-American and Ethiopian Scholars being who will take a significant role in the discussion, the decision will be passed by the current officials of the two countries jointly.

4.1.3 LOCATION OF THE CAPITAL CITY

Where should the capital of the United States of Ethiopia be located? And where should be the seat of the presidency? Is Washington DC going to be the capital of the new state? Or is it Addis Ababa? Or is it going to be another city located in Africa or America?

These questions will be resolved subsequently by the discussions of political scholars. It is only possible to address properly this question by taking in to consideration many technical, political and social issues; therefore it will be decided by extensive research and discussion; however the most important thing is that, the public man ministerial office and most important public head quarters will be fairly distributed in the American and African continents within the new territory.

If I am allowed to say something around this mater, let me put forward my personal suggestion as an individual.

Addis Ababa or one of the cities in Africa should be the capital of U.S Ethiopia. The reason is because, It is the fact that present USA has a strong political foundation, its administration system is not prone to any dismember or any loose element; so it is stable and one can't forecast any administrative weakness at the time of the union. On the other hand, the future cities of US Ethiopia located in Africa will be just starting to grow; therefore the future United States of Ethiopia would have a better political stability if the capital city of the new state is established in Addis Ababa or any African State City.

For this reason the foundation of the capital in Africa would be highly beneficial for the political and social rest.

And when we consider the issue from the African Union context, the seat of the African Union is in Addis Ababa. The future United States of Ethiopia's capital foundation in Addis Ababa or in one of the other cities of the current Ethiopia would be useful to consolidate and foster the African Union. Therefore I think that it will be more preferable if the capital city of United States of Ethiopia is in Africa.

4.1.4. The Name Of The State

A question may be raised that this state being named 'United States of Ethiopia' bolsters Ethiopia's name; but, it will not make the name of US-America to continue as previously as it does not incorporate in it the name 'America'. Will the people and government of US-America consent to the naming of the union as indicated above?

This question, no doubt, can be raised. Basically, the name by which US-America is currently known <u>(United States of America)</u> indicates that different states found in the American continent being administered by one central government having formed a union.

If the current US-America incorporates additional states found in Africa, it will not be appropriate if this country is known as "US-America"; this is because, local states which are part of the main state will exist not only in the American continent but in Africa as well. Rather, it should be named '<u>United States of America and Africa</u>'. However this name since it is lengthy; it will not be simple to be pronounced unless it is abbreviated.

The second weak point of the name '<u>United States of America and Africa</u>' is that it will require to be changed if this state in the future incorporates other states from other continents other than America and Africa for example in Asia or in Oceania.

To the contrary, the name 'Ethiopia' is not a name based on the continent. Therefore if ever Ethiopia has a region crossing its current geographic location, the name Ethiopia will not cause any problem to it; because the name Ethiopia is not issued having as its base the continent, a certain specific area or based on a certain place.

Since the name Ethiopia is given not limited to a particular area, it can cover any desired area. But since the name US-America is based on the continent (or on a certain place) it is limited to a certain area.

Since the United States of Ethiopia which will be established on the absolute union of US-America and Ethiopia will have property and land holding both in the American and the African continents its naming should not be limited over a certain area.

There is an opportunity that this state can have additional territories in other continents meaning in Asia, Oceania and Europe. Strongly urging to expedite the process which leads to the unity of our world to continue at a faster pace, and when the world is led by one state administration and then since a Global Government will be established, I will suggest until then the name 'United States of Ethiopia' to have an acceptance,

The other factor is that the name Ethiopia is antique and that it is a name having a reputable place in ancient scriptures as well as religious books. And this name has to be considered as world heritage and that it is a name whose sovereignty should be made sustain.

The name America is also a name very highly honorable and historical and should be treasured forever. Now and in the future the north and South American continents will be called by this name.

The new state being named' United States of Ethiopia' will not restrict the continuity of the name of America. Since this state is found in America and Africa, the name 'America' will continue as a name of the continent.

Thirdly, the opinion I shall present under this caption, when Ethiopia and US-America establish a Union is since the political and administration structure falls under the current US-American government, this situation will not bring any type of psychological change in the part of Americans.

However, since Ethiopians are going to get introduced to a new type of administrative structure, they must feel that it is a phenomenon that is developed to improve their olden nation but not that it has come to change their Ethiopian identity with a new one. The name 'Ethiopia' is considered as an expression ones identity in the minds of the majority of Ethiopians. This name being made to continue as it is, as long as it does not harm Americans and since it will make Ethiopians to feel a high morale, why won't it be so? I will wind up this way my idea on the naming of the state.

4.1.5 THE NATIONAL LANGUAGE

A question may be raised as to which language would serve as the national and working language. English language should be the national language in the new state. The reason is such that this language is spoken by a number of people and that it has had international influence.

Today, a number of languages are being spoken in the U.S.A. Some of these languages serve as working languages at the specific places where their native speakers live. However, the national language is English.

Now a day, there are quite a number of languages in Ethiopia and any part of the society or individuals are entitled to express themselves using their mother tongue. However, a common language must be in use to ensure that segments of the society would communicate with one another. For example, Amharic language is used in the City of Addis Ababa for all segments of the society to communicate with one another. English language, in turn, is considered to be the language that should be spoken by everyone and it is thought to all students at schools.

English language has significantly considerable acceptance both by Americans and Ethiopians.

Hence, English language should serve the national language of the United States of Ethiopia to be formed in the future and the other languages should serve as working languages in the localities where their speakers are found in large numbers.

4.1.6 THE NATIONAL FLAG

The Ethiopian people love their flag having the green, yellow and red colors. The same is true for the American people and government. Therefore, which flag is to be used when the two countries unite and form the United States of Ethiopia? Which country's flag is to be discarded? These are possible questions that may be raised.

It is true that both the people of America and that of Ethiopia love their flags. It is not believed that it would be difficult for designers or artists to come up with design in which both of the flags are represented or comprised. It is expected from the professionals to come up with a beautiful flag that comprises the flags of both Ethiopia and the United States of America.

Even though Ethiopians have been using the green, yellow and red flag, various governments have used various emblems in the middle of the flag. For example, there was the picture of the lion at the reign of His Imperial Majesty Haile Selassie I. In the current administration, there is the symbol of the star. Even though the flag of green, yellow and the red colors has been used as the representation of the Ethiopian people, it is not new for Ethiopians to witness various emblems being attached with the flag.

When the union of Ethiopia and the United States is realized, there will be flag that comprises the flags of both Ethiopia and the United States. This shall be prepared by artists with the required profession and shall be used upon the approval of the government of the Union.

4.1.7 THE LEGAL CURRENCY

The question "which currency shall be applicable for the United States of Ethiopia" may be raised. The currency of the US Ethiopia State should be the current American Dollar. As we know, there cannot be two types of different national currencies within one country.

As the Ethiopian Birr is devaluating at expedited rate, the exchange rate of 1 dollar is more than 16 Ethiopian Birr. Hence, in the future state of US Ethiopia, Ethiopian currency will not be used. However, the existing American dollar will continue as the currency of the United States. Ethiopians and Americans who shall have been the citizens of the newly formed union would need to transact in dollars and Ethiopians having the Ethiopian birr notes would need to exchange their money in to equivalent notes of the dollar currency.

4.1.8 PREREQUISITE

When the governments of US-America and Ethiopia decide to establish US-Ethiopia what is expected that they would give priorities for and that they would set preconditions?

It is evident that US-America and Ethiopia will produce their prerequisites before they come into agreement to put into practice this theory.

In order for Ethiopians to agree on the theory, what will they need from the American government? And what will Americans need from the Ethiopian government to agree on the issue?

It is basically the responsibility of the governments of the two countries to identify and present to negotiation what their prerequisites are.

What I would like to say on this topic is, to give a positive criticism on this theory, to fulfill its gaps and to develop it, afterwards to put it into practice being the utmost responsibility of the elites and government officials of the two countries; because they are the final decision makers.

4.1.9 IMPLIMENTATION

Should the question about the processes involve in the transformation would be raised, the answer would be as follows:

First of all this theory will be studied by Ethiopian and American intellectuals and deliberations and consultations shall be held. Then the plan will be developed and improved having incorporated the criticisms of various intellectuals. The governments of the two states will meet and study the theory on their own accord and shall make their own evaluations. Then the two governments will conclude an irreversible covenant between themselves and they will form governmental structure. The next activity would be to issue the same kind of ID card to the entire peoples of Ethiopia and America and to provide social security number to each individual citizen. Any person holding such ID card shall be authorized to move to any place within the territory as well as work and live in any part of the newly formed state. A number of investors who have American background from various parts of the countries close to the state would come in to united state. They shall establish various and many factories, hospitals, various business organizations, research centers and etc and they shall provide job opportunities for the jobless. The amount of salary to be paid to the employees shall be above the minimum amount to be determined by the government. They shall be saved from any labor abuse whatsoever.

On the other hand, those persons from the countries around the Unified State in Africa shall have the chance to go to the territories of the union found in the continent of America. They will engage in any field of work they wish and they will have the chance to excel in way of life.

The people of the two nations shall have larger places if they unite and form a single nation. They shall also have diverse job opportunities; and would also be contented.

In the new state, the private organizations, religious institutions, business firms, "Eders" and Associations as well as other nongovernmental organizations shall continue to exist as they are. The governmental offices in Ethiopia shall continue to exist but their accountability will be to the central government of the newly formed state structure.

The officials who are currently engaged in official government positions shall continue to hold certain posts in the new government of the United States of Ethiopia. Even though the administrative structure would follow the same trend as the one in the current United States of America, the government officials of Ethiopia shall hold various ministerial offices and other authorities based on their abilities and skills even though they may not have the same titles as before. As such they shall hold certain senior and junior positions. As the current local states in Ethiopia require administrators and as it is preferable if the administrators belong to the same societies, some of the high rank government officials shall hold positions in administrating the local states while others shall be appointed as mayors of cities while still others shall be appointed in various posts as government high officials.

Civil servants that had been serving before the unification of the two nations should all continue to hold their jobs. There should not be any deduction of salary or benefits. However, some changes in regards to job positions may be introduced. Moreover, the concerned individual may be required to work at a different position with certain change of his title.

No deduction on the benefits earned by any person or segment of the society should be made after the realization of the theory.

The realization of this theory should not be partially benefiting and partially disadvantageous. Rather, it should be beneficial for all.

4.1.10 THE NEXT ACTION

What will be the next action of the people and the government after the establishment of the US-Ethiopia?

The tasks of the peoples and the government after the establishment of the US-Ethiopia will be developing the economic, political and social well being of this state and to strive to solve the internal problems.

The strengthening of the positive sides and improving the negative sides being as accepted, the government will make diplomatic efforts for the states of the neighboring countries found in north and south America, the countries of Latin America and the Caribbean countries to join the union.

In a similar manner diplomatic effort will be carried out so that countries found in Africa with geographic proximity to US Ethiopia to join the union. Even though those to be invited for the union primarily will be countries at proximity with US-Ethiopia and which are found in African and the American continents, it does not mean that this invitation for the union will not be extended to countries found in other continents than Africa and America.

Any country in the world provided it is willing to unite with the US-Ethiopia will receive a happy reply of acceptance. The geographic distance will not create an obstacle for the union for countries having been located in any continent or in any part of the world. The main point is the agreement to be reached between the countries.

This process indicated above, will encourage and support the effort by which our world becomes one. A significant effort has to be made for the world to become one. It has become long since members of the European Union have strengthened their union and are using the 'Euro' as their common currency. They are seen jointly working at higher level in other political and economic issues. What we can realize from this reality is that European countries are traveling to insure unity. This is really an impressive condition.

The African countries as well by establishing a union are undertaking tasks that will enable them for their unity. What Africans and Europeans are undertaking is for a unity it is a thing to be encouraged. It is because the union is made among countries to support and enhance the process whereby the world can become one.

The future policy of the US-Ethiopia union is something to be encouraged as it supports and enhances the process by which our world will become one.

Hence, these activities will be the future tasks of the government.

CHAPTER FIVE
5.1 ADVANTAGES TO BE ACQAIRED BY THE TWO COUNTRIES

5.1.1 THE GAIN OF ETHIOPIANS

The establishment of the United States of Ethiopia is a tremendously high benefit for the present Ethiopians and the future generation.

In fact, we know that our country Ethiopia is now economically progressing as compare to the earlier time. However, Ethiopia is still found among the developing countries.

Due to the economic and technological gap of the country and the lack of economic capacity of its people, our country Ethiopia is quoted as an example of one of the "poorest" countries of the world. Ethiopia has no problem of natural resources. It is an affluent land endowed with a broad population and proprietor of extensive amount of natural resources.

In fact, Ethiopia is now economically progressing. However, for many years, some appalling customary practices impediment of growth that deeply rooted among the society, the fact that there was a bad allocation of natural resources and man power management, and the negative influence of external forces, have slowed down the development of the country. If these three problems are relieved, our country can reach a high stage of development.

Today a great number of Ethiopians are found out of their country and they want to change their way of life by increasing their livelihood. It is not because they want to live far away from their home land; but because they believed that it is better to develop their income working in developed countries. The fact of opting for exodus to live and work is way of life selected by our country men and women against their will and scores of others are dreaming about this alternative without their wish.

Today numerous Ethiopians are living as workers in the USA and although many others are craving to go to America, only a few of them are "successful" since the opportunity is not easily available. Thus, secondly they attempt to emigrate in other countries with better standard than Ethiopia. Today myriads of Ethiopians exist almost all over the world. And our female sisters are constantly going to Arab countries in continuous influx. But only few of them have a good fate. If they are "lucky", wherever they go they may become 2nd rate citizens but never 1st rate citizens.

Exile is the biggest problem of Ethiopians. In some countries where Ethiopians are migrating, they are extremely exploited. Many Ethiopians graduated college and universities have not the opportunity to work in their training area.

Today the proper tackle of the basic needs of mankind is not a worrying issue in developed countries. But in underdeveloped countries such as Ethiopia, the problem of sufficient food, clothing, shelter (housing), health care, education, job, and the like is a topic of discussion. Likewise, in the health field, the third world peoples are condemned to misery and death due to default of health care.

We Ethiopians are not short of natural resources and land space and we have a large man power; so why should we be called "poor" eternally? Most Ethiopians are overlooking the time when they can slate their knowledge and benefit to others through their work. It is not only that, we envision live in improved justice system and a better protection of human rights. We are looking forward to the time when the title of 'poor people' will be removed away from us. It should not be expected that this time is remote. It is possible to reach it in a way of short cut within a short time,

The establishment of the United States of Ethiopia is a way of short cut for us to solve this problem. An individual who works in the United States of Ethiopia is in his/her own country in which ever city he/she is. The right to be not only in any one of the regional states (cities) of current Ethiopia, but also in any local state (city) of US America will be recognized and the citizenship is to be acquired. That citizenship is to be first rate citizenship.

When the Ethiopians and Americans make absolute union, they will form a new unprecedented people. Their borders will be broader their population will be more numerous, their opportunities will rise and their positive influence in the political, social and economic aspects will be much stronger than ever; that is so isn't the establishment of US Ethiopia beneficial to Ethiopians? It is indeed so much beneficial.

5.1.2 Is U. S. America Extremely Commended?

Although United States of America is the first developed country of the world, it is not indicated in this essay for America having a perfect political and administrative structure. The current America is not supposed to be a country having absolutely good political and administrative structure.

Numerous political, social, administrative and even economic problems in US-America have existed and will exist also in the future.

We are living on earth not in heaven. And while living on earth, we don't have to expect a country to exist with an absolutely good system of political, economic and administrative aspects.

However, this does not mean that the administrators of each country being of worldly origins should not correct and improve their problems. Peoples and government of each country should be able to curb the problems of their countries and should develop their nations as much as possible.

While US-America is compared with developing countries similar to Ethiopia, it is found in a much better position in terms of political, economic and technological advancement. Beyond for its own, it is seen supporting other countries.

And while also compared with other developed nations, US-America is found at first grade in its growth and economy. But it does not mean that the country has not problem. This is what is being described in this essay.

Even though solving the internal problems of US-America is mainly the responsibility of the peoples and the government of US-America, secondly all the peoples and governments of the world should not equally forget by developing our countries, our ultimate goal to be developing the world.

When US-Ethiopia is founded, the current peoples of US-America and Ethiopia will work together to develop their state (country) by becoming cohesive. All of the people will work together the social and political problems reflected in the administration of the state.

5.2. THE GAIN OF AMERICANS

US-Americans being currently people who have a country which is developed in the economic and technological sector, on the other hand, Ethiopia being developing in its economy and civilization, how will the Americans volunteer their state to be united with such a developing country?

The establishment of United States of Ethiopia is highly beneficial to present Americans and the future generations.

In present Ethiopia there is a high amount of natural resource. Its weather is conducive and its soil is arable therefore any one can live harmoniously in the environment of Ethiopia. In Ethiopia a large quantity of natural resources inaccessible to colonialists and untapped minerals are available.

If the current USA possesses this wealth, it will be benefitted from it. Nowadays, USA is draining every year a potent man power from the Third World. This shows that America needs an extensive man power.

Today in Ethiopia there is plenty of man power and Ethiopians are migrating to various countries to work physically and intellectually. Therefore when United States of Ethiopia is founded, there will be no shortage of man power. Many investors will flow from America to Africa. They will work in the present Ethiopia, provide with job opportunity and will take advantage from the land and natural resources; in this manner, Americans will be more beneficiaries; their positive influence in the political, social and economic aspects will be much stronger than ever; that is Rehoboth.Moreover, when the United States of Ethiopia is set up, USA will be a member of the African Union and that will permit America to have a positive effect on African politics. May be the USA will have a great positive influence in the unification of the African continent. Accordingly North America, South America and Africa will have conducive conditions to be administered under one state and central government.

5.2.1 WILL IT BE CONSENTED BY AMERICANS ?

It is true that US-America is economically politically and technologically developed. And it is true that Ethiopia to the contrary in the three aspects not developed. However, the Union of these two countries is something that benefits US-Americans but not something that causes problem for them. When US-America establishes Union with Ethiopia, it will obtain the following four great advantages.

1. Additional land
2. Additional natural resource
3. Additional productive human resource
4. Peaceful political gain

Let me elaborate below these four points

1. ADDITIONAL LAND

US-America is a country which has no problem of land. We know that it has land property that places it as 2nd or 3rd place globally.

However, if an opportunity surfaces, that will enable it to get additional land property than it has now, it is impossible to think that is will retreat not to hold on to the additional property.

We are living today in the world where problems on boundaries and conflicts are arising everywhere. What we should realize is that land is not a thing that would be considered to be mentioned as 'enough' in the part of governments.

If US-America makes the current vast land of Ethiopia as the part of its territory no one will have doubt as to US-America becoming the beneficiary out of this.

Additional land will give U-S America numerous benefits. For example it will help it for Agriculture, to build huge industries, factories, research centers and huge real estates.

In addition to this, US America will be able to erect observatory or reconnaissance bases in Africa which in turn will help it make positive impact in the global politics.

2. ADDITIONAL NATURAL RESOURCE

Ethiopia is a country which has a huge untapped natural resource. It is true that US-America currently has a huge natural wealth within its territory. However, if it will have additional natural resource than what it currently has, it will become more beneficiary. A government which says 'what I have is enough' is not observed in our world to-date.

We are living in a world where numerous conflicts are carried out every where as a result of the rush for natural resources.

US-America will benefit if it will possess the current Ethiopian natural resource and tourist attractions alongside with their full rights and privileges.

3. ADDITIONAL PRODUCTIVE HUMAN RESOURCE

Even though joblessness is from time to time manifested in US-America there are indications that this country requires additional human resource. Because of its desires for a productive work force to migrate to its hinterland it is providing resident permits annually to numerous foreigners. Ethiopians are amongst those receiving free invitations (diversity visas).

Many Ethiopians as long as they are productive and lucky to win a diversity lottery then travel to US-America and they work and live there.

The fact that the existence of many Ethiopians who are productive, professionals and skilled is a thing that satisfies the manpower need of US-America and provides it with a great benefit.

4. PEACEFUL POLITICAL GAIN

If US-America's attainment of the highest stage of development in our world attracts the attention of many other countries to be a part of this great state, this situation will decrease the number of other governments which are posing threats to it.

If the superpowers of our world could co-exist peacefully is good. But if this is not possible, they would enter into a non-constructive rivalry and they would try to out win one another with the types and quantities of armaments they produce. They carry out these activities not only by making undeveloped countries become their satellites/ supporters; but also they would make the world to be divided in to two even more groups. We can consider the cold war and other historical conflicts as example to this,

If it happens this way, as the governments of other countries and nations will cooperate with the country that becomes superpower; their good relations with the US America may not continue as it is now.

The Union of Ethiopia and US-America will be decreased by one pace the well being of nations who may undertake political activities out of the interest of the American government. This is one of the political advantages to be gained.

The other is that when US-America will have a territory in Africa the impact it will create in the African political scenario is not something to be considered as easy.

Addis Ababa is the seat of the African Union. When Addis Ababa becomes part of the United States of America there will be no doubt that America will have a greater role in the AU. This is what is meant by political victory.

For these reasons USA can definitely agree with Ethiopia to establish the United States of Ethiopia and no doubt that both peoples will benefit from these initiatives.

CHAPTER SIX
Debatable Issues

6.1 Colonization Or Union?

Among the issues that can be raised in my opinion, "how can the merger of these two countries be different from colonialism?

Colonialism is the aggression of nation to dominate it by force and to exploit it. In colonial administration citizens in the colonized country are considered as 2nd rate citizens. The citizens of the colonized country can't travel freely to the colonist country. Moreover the places where they move are restricted by their masters. Relatively the colonialist country citizens are fully using their rights in the colonized country and it is a system where racism is practiced largely. In the colonial system the colonized has not the right to take part in to politics.

On the other hand the colonialists are exploiting the natural resources of the colony. In general colonialism is characterized by exploitation racism and lack of justice; therefore it is rejected by the whole world. Personally I also condemn this unjust order.

The United State of Ethiopia is established in absolutely different manner. Since, it is the absolute union of two countries. The citizens of this state enjoy their legitimate rights equally. In the areas located in the state administration, one can move, live, work, be involved in politics, elect, and be elected, without restriction and all human rights without reduction are secured. In this state, all peoples will have one constitution and one legislation. Therefore, it is radically different from colonialism.

6.2 WHY IS AMERICA CHOSEN?

There are numerous countries in the world. From among these nations, there are nations that are close in geographical proximity to Ethiopia, such as the African countries, neighboring nations and those that demonstrate cultural similarity. Hence, what is the need to establish Union with the United States of America while this country is far and separated from us by large water bodies and a number of countries? If at all there is the need to establish union, shouldn't it be with those countries in the same continent and with those of the neighboring nations? These questions may be raised, of course.

Ethiopia is a developing country in terms of economical and developmental aspects. The neighboring nations are not much better in these respects in comparison with Ethiopia. Union with such developing countries is rather questionable. The reason is because there is a need to have stable and strong economic and political relations between the countries to form unions. The question as to what administrative codes are to be implemented is also a question that is not easily addressable.

It is easy for developed countries to form unions. However, it is rather difficult for undeveloped countries to form unions. The union that could be formed between Ethiopia and the United States is a lot simpler than unions formed with undeveloped nations. The reason is such that USA does have strong and well established political and economic structure which has the advantage of avoiding disintegration and dismembering of administration.

Geographical location would not be a problem as well. The reason is such that political and administrative strength would surpass the geographical farness. However, where there are political problems, even a small nation may disintegrate rather than maintaining unity.

One of the reasons that led me in to choosing the United States of America is such that America is the first superpower in terms of economy, politics and very much advanced in technological inventions as well.

The second reason that led me in to choosing the United States of America is the other reality that U S A is similar to Ethiopia in terms of the diversity of ethnic groups and races that live together; and hence, it would not be difficult to unite the two countries. However, it would pave the way for disputes and non-belongingness between peoples if unity were to be formed between Ethiopia and a country with white race only. Hence, in consideration of the settlements of the Ethiopian and the American people marked by diversity as well as the fact that the countries are not home for a single race, the union that could be formed between the two nations would doubtlessly be effective.

6.3 CAN THE GEOGRAPHICAL PROBLEM BE A HINDRANCE?

Presently there is a long distance between America and Ethiopia where as a vast space is covered by water. As there are seas and oceans, there is a great disparity between the Geographical positions of the countries. Then how is it possible to unite those countries in one state and one political administration where as there is a great geographical position disparity?

The Geographical position remoteness could be a political problem in ancient times. In the present 21st century, thanks to modern science and technology, remote political administration is no more a problem

Currently we have overwhelming communication and transport utilities such as modern planes, ships, the access to telephone, fax, Internet and E-mail and many advanced discoveries generated by modern science and technology. Today, man is even wishing to live in other planets beyond the Earth and the exploration is going on in expedite fashion. It is not stunning to reach the moon and to come back in the 2nd millennium.

Accordingly in the future union of USA and Ethiopia it is not plausible to think that remoteness would be a political problem.

6.4 THE ISSUE OF CULTURE

We Ethiopians have tremendously reach culture of which we take pride. We have distinctive values in terms of calendar, code of dressing occasional to holidays, cultural foods as well as music and art which distinguish us from other countries. The living style of the people by itself constitutes various traditions. For example, there is the tradition of helping one another and sharing times of happiness and sorrow. It is in Ethiopia that we find institutions such as *"Eder", "Equb"* and associations that have developed through time since the ancient times.

Hence, the question whether such cultures and traditions would be mixed or would completely be lost may be raised upon the establishment of the United States of Ethiopia.

Today in US America, there are various segments of the society. These peoples immigrated in to America from different parts of the world and those immigrating as such; they have taken their cultures with themselves. However, they have managed to adopt the principle of tolerance of cultural differences and they have bestowed their values upon the future generations.

For instance, there are various peoples such as descendants of the British or Anglo-Saxons, the Dutch, German, Irish, Scottish, Black Americans, Mexicans, Red Indians and others. Even Ethiopian nationals who reside in the United States are quite many in number. Matter-of-factly, there is no such thing as American Ethnic identity in the United States of America. The reason is such that the country constitutes various ethnicities in which case we do not find distinct culture that is typical to the United States and that is why the country is referred to as a 'Multicultural' nation.

Even though America is a nation where we find various ethnic identities, there were not circumstances that forced the people to abandon their cultures. Even though the nation is civilized and has adopted modern living style, the people did not need to abandon their culture (tradition) which they believe is beneficial for them.

Similarly, Ethiopia is a nation for various ethnic identities and cultures. There is no such ethnic identity or race denominated Ethiopia. However, tremendously many ethnic groups live together having tolerance to cultural differences of one another. There has never been any situation that has forced the people to abandon their remarkable cultures which have sustained in a number of generations.

There is one important point that is common to both US America and Ethiopia. This important point is that in both countries live people with various ethnic identities and culture. If the two nations form absolute union and establish the United States of Ethiopia, the unified state would be a home for the present Ethiopians, Habeshas and Americans – a country based on differences or diversity of the two peoples. This would allow the two people to live in a country wealthy of technological advancements and natural resources with numerous people, diverse cultures, languages, ethnic identifies and races living in harmony tolerating one another. However, they shall not be forced to abandon their cultures which they consider to be beneficial for them.

6.5 THE QUESTION OF PRIDE

We Ethiopians are proud of our identity; we do not bargain on our sovereignty. Hence, a question may be raised as to how we give up our identity and sovereignty or surrender our country to foreigners.

The realization of the United States of Ethiopia cannot be taken as giving up or surrendering our country to foreigners. The union of the two nations does not mean surrendering one's county to the other. The reason is such that the people of the two countries would have the same nationality and the peoples would have larger sized territory. When both Ethiopians and the Americans become under the same government, they will have a chance to work and reside in the American and African continents.

Moreover, both Ethiopians and Americans shall have the chance to have similar nationalities and hence shall enjoy the advantage of participation in politics and to elect and be elected.

In terms of pride, the chance that Ethiopians would have to inherit the continent of America in addition to the continent of Africa would make them even more proud than otherwise. Hence, the realization of the United States of Ethiopia is not to be in conflict with our national pride. Rather, we Ethiopians herewith would be possessors of a new pride in addition to our existing pride. That is additional honor.Rather, we Ethiopians would be possessors of an additional pride and a new additional honor.

6.6 THE QUESTION OF HISTORY AND HERITAGE

"Ethiopians have their own history and heritage of which they are prodding and which spans back more than 3000 years. Likewise US-Americans have their own history. Would the union of these two countries not bring spoil or turmoil of history?"

It is evident that Ethiopia is a country that has diverse history which is handed over to successive generations. Even though the country has a well-recognized and exemplar stories, it also has appalling stories. If we study each documented fact in the Ethiopian history, we can find good as well as bad stories.

In the same way if US-America's history that has existed to-date is meticulously reviewed, good as well as bad historical data will be revealed.

The two countries, US-America and Ethiopia possess good and bad histories. History is a phenomenon which is performed and recorded during different eras to be handed over to successive generations. But it is not an idol restricted not to be repeated or not to make other histories.

History can be made even today. The history to be made today might be commended or blamed by future generations. Each generation has to make its own good history and has to hand it over to the coming generation.

We the people of this generation have inherited good as well as bad histories from past generations. Both are observed teaching, benefiting and harming us. We would rather make every effort possible to hand over a good history to the next generation than live simply by worshiping history as an idol.

The formation of the United States of Ethiopia is not a fact that tears down the previous histories of the US-America and Ethiopia. The history of Ethiopia is going to be part of the history of United States of Ethiopia; and the history of U.S.A is also going to be part of the history of the United States of Ethiopia. Therefore at the time of the union, Ethiopians' history will become the history of Americans as well. The Americans' history will also become the history of Ethiopians as.

What will become more blissful is that the establishment of the United States of Ethiopia is to be one whole great history. This is a history to be proud of as it is a history that benefits not only the present generation but also the coming one. Let us discharge our responsibility of handing over a reputable work to the coming generation by implementing this theory.

6.7 The Threat Of Migration And Population Explosion

"US-America is a country that has a huge population; Ethiopia is also a country that has huge population. When these two countries unite and establish one state, the population of the new state will have a huge populating constituting the merger of the current population of the two countries. Will this not cause a problem to the Americans? How will Americans challenge the huge population influx of people migrating from Africa (the current Ethiopia) to the US-America? "

Basically, if working opportunities and conditions are made appropriate to the Ethiopian people they are people who will work and produce. The number of Ethiopians currently immigrating to different countries and who are gaining an achievement utilizing their labor, knowledge and profession is immense.

The problem for the current Ethiopian to become "poor" is not the natural phenomenon. The problem, however, is related to the

1. Governance problem that was prevalent since many years back,
2. Some armful customary practices and attitudes that are deeply rooted in the society,
3. Conflicts that ravaged the country from time to time
4. Negative impacts against the country imposed by foreigners directly or indirectly.

* If the problems mentioned here are solved, Ethiopians beyond benefiting themselves, they can become productive and even will be able to aid others.

While these problems are problems of Ethiopians, even though it is hard to say that US-Americans are hundred percent free from such problems, it is evident that they live in a much better and higher condition.

When Ethiopia and US-America establish a Union, the drawbacks prevalent within the two countries will be fulfilled a better pace and condition.

Since Ethiopians will get employment opportunities, they will utilize their accumulated knowledge and potential in the employment they are offered. They will develop the new great state with their American brothers in unison.

A condition will not prevail that will make Africans or the majority of the current Ethiopians to leave behind their domicile and to travel to the United States.

A human being naturally does not desire to leave beyond its birth place and to migrate to distant places leaving behind the weather it is adapted to and the vicinity where his/her next kith and kin are at proximity unless forced by a problem or special circumstance.

During the Union, the majority of the Ethiopians provided they get conducive working and living environment they will not prefer to live far from their birth area.

Since any American or Ethiopian becomes a citizen of the new great state at the time of the Union, even though he/she has the right for movement, work and residence in any region (city) of the state, will be ascertained a citizen using these rights will move from one place to another only on his/her preference.

Let me explain the reasons which I said would decrease the huge influx of people from one to another area: when the united state of Ethiopia will be established:-

- The government offices currently operative in the Ethiopian government, at the time of the US-Ethiopia Union, since they will be accountable to the main state government structure, these organizations will have an equal status growth with government offices of US-America. The salaries they pay for their employees being in dollar and will be paid on the basis of the scales of the current US-government. Therefore there will not be a reason that government employees found in Ethiopia to quit their jobs and to travel to America. This is because they will not get better income by going there. This condition will help peoples' migration not to be exasperated

- The other factor is that most of the employees currently working in various private and public organizations will not abandon their living areas and travel to the United States. This is because the working system of the current government offices will be equal to the standard prevalent in the US today and this condition will also be reflected upon the working conditions of private companies. Since the rules and regulations by which non-governmental offices are administered at that time will

37

follow government laws, it will be the same with the policies by which private companies are currently administered in the US-America. Non-governmental organizations which will be operational at that time in America and in Africa (the current Ethiopia) will not have a high salary scale difference. And this means the non-governmental worker with a lesser salary scale in the state's cities in Africa will not be lesser than the organization with minimal salary scale in America. Since the development that will prevail in the country will make beneficial non-governmental offices and working stations, and because it will enable the organizations to raise their salary scales, they will pay what is required by their employees. If they don't do this, as their employees will quit their jobs the employers will be forced to handle their employees properly in order not to lose their employees. And this condition also will prevent people from migrating from Africa to America.

• The number of US-Ethiopian governmental offices in Africa will increase. Both existing and new ones. Since the manpower requirement of the organizations likewise increases, new employment opportunities will be available. This being one factor, since the current companies in the US-America will establish their branch offices in the cities of the state found in Africa and since this also will make job opportunities for the current Ethiopians the number of people traveling from Africa to America will decrease.

In addition to this, taking into consideration the favorable weather and living conditions prevalent in the current Ethiopia, big companies of the current US-America engaged in real estate business will start operating in Africa (current Ethiopia) subsequent to the establishment of US- Ethiopia. This condition will provide work opportunities for a number of Ethiopian companies and workers engaged in construction activities and this will also greatly decrease the number of the people migrating to the continent of America.

The other factor is that, in US-America there exist numerous types of service areas, occupational disciplines (fields of profession); but in Ethiopia it is quite few types of occupational disciplines are known. Several of those who are currently found in US-America and engaged in various investment and other activities will come to the current Ethiopia at the time of the establishment of the US-Ethiopia in order to introduce their services.

The reason is that most of the jobs they carry out are familiar in America and when they start doing it in a place where it is not well known previously, it will make them profitable. This means market completion is high in America but law in Ethiopia.

For this reason the number of Americans coming to Africa (Ethiopia) being huge and since in turn will create additional job opportunities for people in Ethiopia it will greatly reduce the migration of people to America.

The other factor is that the number of Americans traveling from America to Africa (the current Ethiopia) for various reasons will balance the number of people traveling from Africa to America.

As the points I raise above decrease the influx of people from one place to another the number of current Ethiopians migrating to America leaving behind their domicile will not be that much threatening.

It could be for one reason that other Ethiopians will travel to America which will not be forced to remain home for reasons indicated above. And this is because they think they do a better job and get a better pay. And people who travel with this idea must be more productive. If these productive peoples go to America, they will benefit not only themselves but also other peoples through their work.

The majority of the Ethiopian current population constitutes the youth. The elderly are few in number. For reasons I described above, if the problem of the youth can be solved, the problem of the elderly and children will not remain unsolved. The reason is that in a country if the youth is productive, the results of its products no doubt will also reach children and the elderly.

I assume to have provided sufficient reply to the question about the threat of migration and population explosion.

6.8 THE ISSUE OF RACE, ETHNICITY
AND LOSS OF IDENTITY

"Ethiopians and Americans have their own race and ethnic identities. Will the union of the peoples of these two countries not make them loose in the future their identity? "

As we have observed in other sections of this essay, US-America and Ethiopia are countries where different races and ethnic groups are living as one and where the unity of the people in diversity is reflected.

If we look at the condition in Ethiopia, we can observe the inter marriage among different members of ethnic groups and that they are bringing new generations with new identities.

Even though some individuals exist who discourage the mixing of their race with others through marriage, most Ethiopians are, however, making practical the marriage with other Ethiopian ethnic group members and have began creating an extended union among peoples.

For example the people living in the capital city, Addis Ababa, are people who are constituted from different mingled races/ethnic people. Most of the Youth of Addis Ababa are not that seriously bothered about their original ethnicity being whether or not mixed with other ethnic groups/races.

This is because they have come maintaining new identities. It is a natural process for people coming more together and to create a similar psychological makeup, similar culture and consciousness. This condition is something that existed ones and will exist in the future too.

Ethiopians in addition to the good ethnic relationship and closer ties they are establishing amongst themselves they are also observed establishing relationships with people outside of their country. And this condition today has created numerous multiracial Ethiopian citizens.

In my opinion I believe being born multicultural has advantages. A person who is multicultural is less racist. Our world today does not benefit from racism. Instead each of us should develop the sense of humanity and need to lead the world towards one direction.

If the sources of ethnic originality of all of us could be examined properly going backwards in history, our main source is one.

The color difference i.e. white, black, brown seen amongst us is a different that has surfaced after centuries. The entire human race has come from one source many centuries ago.

For example, if a person goes to a hospital, for medical or surgical reason or as a result of an accident or sickness, and if he/she is required to have blood donation, he/she will have the chance of surviving as long as a person is available that can donate blood.

Therefore, the person that provides the blood donation, if he/she comes from any one race or ethnic group does not pose a problem. Biological scientists divide the human blood in four groups. They are: 'A' Group, 'B' Group, 'AB' Group and 'O' Group. These blood groups are not limited to one but are found in any race or ethnic group.

There is no scientific limitation that states the blood donation to be provided to the patient mentioned above should come from a certain race or ethnic group. The blood of a white prson will be suitable for a black person. The blood of a black person will as well be suitable for a white person. In contrast, the blood of another species of animal will never become suitable to another species of animal.

For example if a person does not get a blood donation from another person a blood from a non-human animal will not be provided. It is because the animal's species is utterly different from the human species.

Biological laboratory technicians can differentiate animal's blood from human blood. However, they cannot ascertain which blood belongs to which race by testing bloods collected from different races.

What we shall understand from this is that all human beings have similar blood. Why we human beings have similar blood is because our origin is one.

Therefore, if the origin of our race is one where does the difference being observed today in our color, height, hair etc come from? This is an impact made on the human race as a result of living and adapting to different cultures and places in our world. And also it emanated as a result of different weather conditions and geographic locations.

Even though the above factors have created dissimilarity amongst the human race, since our origin is the same we are all brothers and sisters. Instead of promoting ethnicity and racism among ourselves, let us promote humanity.

I will say the ethnic mixing being carried out in Ethiopia through marriages and birth between different ethnic peoples and foreigners is something good and need to be encouraged to sprout from time to time.

Even though I respect as a belief the outlook of some individuals who oppose this principle, but since I differ from them in terms of idea, I encourage the mixing of race and ethnicity to that the people of our world at the end will become multiracial.

People living in US-America are creating a multi-cultural and multi racial people similar to that of Ethiopia by creating relationships with others through friendship, marriage and by crating closeness as well as creating similar ideology psychological makeup. In my opinion this condition is something that makes one happy.

There is nothing that forces the peoples of America and Ethiopia to mix their race or ethnic group or to get married to another race or ethnic group. This is purely done based on the interest of the individuals. That is why when some limit their marriage only to the ethnic group of their own; others go beyond that since this is a matter purely based on the interests of individuals.

When US-Ethiopia will be formed there will not be a different thing than what has been described above. If there will be a person or society that would want one's ethnicity (race) not to be mixed with others they can do this on their own merit and can teach others and can pass over to others their principle. But he can do this only in a way that it does not affect the interests of others.

However an individual, who has not the filling of ethnicity and racism, does not have much worry about the mingling or not of a particular race with another.

Since I don't also have a feeling of racism and ethnicity, it is not something that worries me much. In my opinion, what is more important for us human beings is to foster humanity and the feeling of brotherhood amongst ourselves.

6.9 THE QUESTION OF RACISM

"When US-Ethiopia is established, will the feeling of racism, discrimination and isolation exist or not?"

Earlier as we have observed in other sections of this paper, Ethiopia and US-America are countries where different races and ethnic group are living together as one and where the diversity of people is reflected in their unity. When these countries are united, it is not expected that a feeling of serious racist sentiment will surface. However it is expected that some problems may be encountered in this respect.

A problem of this type of small magnitude, even though it is reflected by some individuals for a short time, the problem will be solved through time.

Even though numerous ethnic groups are living in Ethiopia, it is not possible to assert the fact that their national rights were properly and equally observed from long ago. Some ethnic groups have lived as superiors to the others for a long time.

Even though it is not possible to assert that a similar problem of this nature to have been eradicated fully from Ethiopia, when compared from olden times, it is found to be in a much better stance. And for in the future, similar problems of this sort are expected to decrease and one day to be eradicated altogether.

History attests in a similar manner that there existed a serious black and white racial discrimination in the olden US-America. This problem is being solved from time to time and today they are found at a highly improved situation. Even though we cannot confidently say that similar problem does not currently exist in US-America, it is evident that the current American people are found at a much better position than the previous one.

And there will not be a reason why a problem of this sort would not be solved completely in the future.

When Ethiopia and US-America agree and establish the 'United States of Ethiopia', even though a small race discrimination that could be evident at that time would be reflected by some individuals, similar problems would be eradicated in the long run.

We can understand from the Ethiopian and US-American objective reality that we were able to see as described above, the problem of racism and discrimination is a thing that gradually becomes eroded and in the long term to be eradicated altogether.

When two and above people who are of different history of race and ethnicity and who have different cultural background, when they start building similar ideology and similar psychological makeup and when they strengthen their relationship through inter marriages and birth this will make the coming generation free from the feeling of racism..

Therefore, when US-Ethiopia will be established similar problem will not be that much bothering.

6.10 Opportunities For Ethiopian Government Officials

"It is described that the current US-American government administration will continue as it is now. Then, what is going to be the future kismet of the Ethiopian government officials?"

At the time of the establishment of the United States of Ethiopia the name of the US-American government will be modified and will be known as "US-Ethiopian Government". The current Ethiopian government officials will also work in the US-Ethiopian government offices at different levels. It will not be required for any officials of the Ethiopian government to be expelled from his/her occupation. They will be working together with officials who have been administering the US-America.

Since numerous offices of the state prevail in Africa and America which will undertake various government activities and since the experience of Ethiopian officials will provide a huge benefit, they will work in the different offices. Above this, some of the current Ethiopian government officials who have vast knowledge and experience will have the opportunity to work as senior advisors and managers in the governmental offices of US-Ethiopia to be established in the future.

Even though the Ethiopian government officials will stay at their work at that time it may not be with the present position that they have now that they shall continue. Since their salaries and benefits will be with the US Standard, it is evident that they will be better beneficial that what they are currently earning. However they can be assigned to different positions and they may encounter transfer, promotions as well as demotions.

There is one point to be realized here; if we take the least minimum salary currently being paid by US-America to government officials and if we compare it to the salary and benefit paid to higher officials currently by the Ethiopian government the least salary the Americans are paid is more than what the Ethiopian officials are paid. At the establishment of the US Ethiopia even though any government official is employed at a junior level since he/she will get better benefit that what is given to him/her currently working at a senior level he/she should not feel threatened for what will happen at the time of the union. And when one officials of the United States of Ethiopia is retired with pension after completing the tenure of office, since she/he will get legal benefits as per what is being practiced in the current US-American government, his/her benefits will not in any way be jeopardized.

6.11 THE QUESTION OF HIERARCHY

"**A** human being is a creature that naturally requires demonstrating supremacy. In the opinions presented in this theory when US-Ethiopia will be established, it is the Americans that will occupy the senior positions in the political field for a certain period of time. Even though the current Ethiopian government officials will continue to work occupying senior positions and that the legal benefits they earn will improve, since there is a possibility that they will not get their current senior positions, how will they satisfy their desires of Political Superiority?"

Before I give a reply to this question first I would like to seize this opportunity to convey a message.

The efforts being made by the current senior government officials of Ethiopia to develop Ethiopia is a thing to be admired and to be supported. They have to continue their efforts in a more strengthened manner. The Ethiopian people should also strive hard to develop their country by working in collaboration with the government.

I, the initiator/writer of this proposal, support the development activities that the Ethiopian government is currently undertaking and I believe that I shall discharge my responsibilities by working with the government to develop my country.

The reason why I have prepared this write-up (theory) is not as a result of opposing the Ethiopian government policy, but to present an alternative proposal for a very fast development initiative beneficial for my country and because of the desire I have to realize my wish for the unity of the world.

Once I have made this clear, let me provide my answer to the question presented above. It is true that a human being has a desire to become superior. And unless this is supported by positive thinking and objectivity it can become a source of destruction.

Why we men should stay in power should be to discharge our responsibility to serve our nation, our people and generations. But it should not be having the view to become obstacles for development having been blindfolded with the lust for authoritative supremacy.

At the time when US-Ethiopia will be established, even though the current Ethiopian government officials will work together with American officials, since the current American government will continue with its current administrative and political structure, it is expected for a certain period the seniority of the American officials will prevail. It is a fact not to be contested that the Americans will occupy key positions.

This condition as long as it does not harm people; Ethiopian officials should not oppose the practicality of this theory.

We are talking about a theory that will enable our country to become a superpower and the first rich and developed state in the world in only one year time.

I don't really expect the existence of an individual nor group who perceives, 'Instead of me losing authoritative seniority let Ethiopia with its people remain not developed'; but if there exists one it will be good to change his/her opinion of this reflection.

We human beings on individual basis the life time that we have on earth is very short. We will become mistaken being keen for our authoritative life that does not last for long if don't allow for a better alternative not to come that benefits people and the coming generation.

In my opinion I don't assume a government official who has similar negative opinion like this one currently exists in Ethiopia. I believe that the Ethiopian government officials will view positively if an alternative opportunity expediting the fast and reliable development of Ethiopia is forwarded and that they will strive for its practicality.

6.12 THE THREAT OF EXPLOITATION
AND EMBEZZLEMENT

"When US-America will be formed and when the two countries lead jointly the state, it is Americans as well as Ethiopians who will be together holding political positions. However, it is expected that most senior and key positions to be held by Americans.

At that time, probably what is if Americans haul Ethiopian resources and precious historical treasures to their country? Would Theft and embezzlement of the wealth of Ethiopians not be committed at that time? And would such situation not affect Ethiopians?"

The hauling of natural resources in the manner of embezzlement is carried out from one country to another only under colonialism and when the embezzler and the embezzled are two different countries. The Union of US-America and Ethiopia is an absolute union that makes the two countries one.

Since this absolute union makes the two countries one; they will be administered by one Federal Government. Embezzlement of wealth will not be carried out in a country of absolute union.

When US-Ethiopia will be formed, the current Ethiopia will also belong to Americans and America will also belong to Ethiopians,

What we have to remember once again is at the time of the Union the US-America and the Ethiopian people will have similar citizenship.

At the time of the union since the two peoples will become one, if they may transport the resource in Africa (the current Ethiopia) to America, it could be meant to distribute the wealth amongst the people. In a similar manner, a huge resource will be hauled from America to Africa (the current Ethiopia). And this will become an issue of managing the resources but not an issue of embezzlement.

We have to note that at the time of the union, the current Ethiopia becomes the property of Americans and Ethiopians. Americans will not unlawfully embezzle this land which is equally theirs. This is because a person does not steal his/her own property.

6.13 What Kind Of Feeling Will Political Hierarchy Reflect Among The People?

"At that time when the American officials hold most senior and key positions, what will political administrative hierarchy reflect towards the filling of the current Ethiopian People? Won't they be disappointed?"

The majority of Ethiopians, above anything else, need peace and stability. They also need basic things for their livelihood such as enough food health care, better shelter, employment/sufficient income etc. Above this, each citizen needs his/her right to be ascertained in the face of the law.

Since these things will be found in the US-Ethiopia in better extent, it is believed that the current Ethiopians will be satisfied with this.

47

The feeling of racism and the thought of power superiority competition comes after a human being gets first the basic needs.

Since conditions for the current Ethiopians at the time of the establishment of US-Ethiopia will be made available that will allow them to improve their livelihood as well as that they will have different options to satisfy their needs, they will become more pleased. So, they will not worry about the issue from which race the administrators and senior officials would be.

However the question of similar racism and superiority and subordination will be ignited in the feelings of some individuals. And this feeling of racism may be a thing to be thought by some people of the current generation only. In the future when a new generation comes, the feeling of racism becomes limited, and conditions will be created for black Africans or Habeshas who are of black races to occupy senior positions as long as they have the capacity and the knowledge. The important matter is to be able to be found competent.

As an evidence for this, we can consider the African Americans in the current US –America like Barrack Obama, Condoliza Rise, Collin Paul and others who have key political positions.

6.14 Fears For Breaking The Covenant

"It is indicated that when US-Ethiopia will be established the political and administrative structure would continue being similar to what is currently being practiced by US-America; It is evident that key positions will be occupied by American officials for a certain period of time; Therefore, after the union materializes, what is if Americans transport Ethiopian resources and historical heritages (antique treasures) to America and later if they break the promise of the Union? And if they give a statement which says, 'we will no more have a union with Ethiopians henceforth!!' Will this not be harming Ethiopians? How will it be possible to have assurance that such similar affair shall not surface?"

Before a decision is made to put in practice this theory, the governments of Ethiopia and US-America will present their prerequisites. Amongst the prerequisites that these governments present one has to be that will abolish this threat.

In order not to down turn or violate the agreement the agreement to be signed must be one that gives emphasis for this matter. There will be no fear to break the promise since the agreement will be carried out as per the international law and involve the United Nations, the African Union Commission, European Union commission and other internationally recognized institutions as observers.

6.15 POSSIBLE OR IMPOSSIBLE?

"When this theory is viewed as a concept, it looks good. Bur it is not possible to put it in practice. Why is it important to think of a theory which cannot become practical?" Some people may raise this question.

Basically, if one theory is good as a theory it is important to implement it instead of turning it down saying, 'it cannot be practical'. Even though it cannot become practical at the time of its initiation, at least it should be kept as a praiseworthy document to be transferred to the coming generation so that the coming generation shall put it in practice after having made its own revisions/modifications.

There are numerous political theories which are not put into practice but which are kept as praiseworthy documents. For example, Plato's 'The Republic' and 'The Law', Saint Augustine's 'The Two Cities', The idea of Scientific Communism of Marx and Lenin etc. can be cited here. These earlier theories are not thrown as having not being put in practice. Instead they are being studied by political scientists and students are also being encouraged to know them.

Theory is a thing to be changed in practice. The technological results that we observe in our vicinities and the good and bad implications observed within the political spectrum are things which were primarily conceived as theories. A theory based on objectivity if it cannot become practical at one time, it will be practical at another era. Even if it cannot become practical today, it can be maintained as a heritage and can be handed over to generations.

What has to be noticed is whether the theory is beneficial for human beings or not.

This theory is a theory that contains the ideals of all human beings. Above all, I believe that it will highly benefit Ethiopians and Americans.

I don't think that there exists enough proof that will able not to qualify this theory as being not practical. Presenting a proof for the practicality or non-practicality of a theory has to be supported with scientific and logical debates and but with blind folded argument.

We have observed through the questions and answers that have been presented so far about this theory being scientific and logical. I have given sufficient reply to the questions I expected to be raised.

Therefore, if this theory is a theory supported with objectivity/cause and is scientific and logical; and that it benefits the parties which it had presented as key players; and if the stakeholders are these similar parties, why can't it be practical?

This theory is beneficial for Ethiopian peoples and government. Likewise, it is also beneficial for the people and government of US-America. To put the theory in practice, the decisive parties are the peoples and governments of Ethiopia and America. If that is so, there is no reason why the theory cannot be put in practice.

6.16 ABSENCE OF HISTORICAL EXPERIENCE

This theory encompasses two different courtiers located at extremely distant places to unite. However a Union has never been carried out previously between countries located at distant places. So how will this become practical?

It is true such phenomenon has not been so far evidenced in our world. Even though neighborly countries could unite, a union has never been made between countries located in vastly distanced continents. The non-practicability of a previous union in our world should not be presented as an excuse for a union not to be materialized in the future. Our world is changing from time to time. What were impossible long times a go are possible today to be achieved. What cannot be made possible today will become possible in the future. In order to decide the practicality of a theory to become possible or not is its being scientific and beneficial; but the fact that a similar thing did not happen in the past should not be considered as an excuse.

CONCLUSION

What shall then we say? The world should be unified; the peoples who live in the world should be well aware of the fact that they are brothers and sister. It is when the human race comes together and work for a common purpose that we can get rid of hanger, diseases, war, political commotion or instability, deforestation, air pollution, terrorism, crime and other similar undesirable aspects and make our world peaceful and comfortable.

When we look at the creatures of the world from the tiny atom to the gigantic universe, we can understand that they are smaller organizations making part of the big organization.

All creature, were created to establish the big organization by supporting one another. The border demarcations of the world should not make us forget that we are brothers & sisters.

The contents and peoples and governments of the world should work relentlessly to improve their respectively continents. This governments, states and peoples should improve their continents in view of improving the entire world.

We Ethiopians should make our country developed. In doing so our major vision should be to develop Africa and eventually to develop the world.

Our Country Ethiopia can reach significant developmental status when the STATE MERGE APPROACH is made practical. The unification of Ethiopia and America by virtue of absolute merge shall cause other countries of north and South America as well as Caribbean countries (Latin Americans) to unite with the newly formed state considering the suitability of the US Ethiopian geographical location found in American continent. Similarly neighboring nations of the US Ethiopian state and other African nations would be invited to join United States of Ethiopia.

When the countries of North and South American Continents as well as those of Latin America and Caribbean become part of the US Ethiopian territories, it would mean that they will come to be governed under the same state. This situation would allow scoring considerably high points in the endeavors geared towards global unification.

The union created between Ethiopia and US America shall be the key to the union to be created between countries of North and South America and Africa because of their possibility to join the United States of Ethiopia. Ultimately the world will be under one state administration; this will help all human kind be united and able to work for the same goal. That goal is to develop the earth to keep it from any kind of danger.

Hence, Dear peoples and governments of Ethiopia and the United States of America; let us discuss and make this proposal come true.

Your comment towards this book is appreciated.
Abel Andarge
E-mail abel_andarge@yahoo.com
P.O.BOX 70304 Addis Ababa Ethiopia.

www.ingramcontent.com/pod-product-compliance
Lightning Source LLC
Chambersburg PA
CBHW031328290526
45784CB00014B/2421